The Test

'We have a test for you,' Mark and Hannah said. They were her two best friends.

'A test for me? Why? What's it about?' Kara asked.

'Leonardo DiCaprio . . .'

'Oh, my favourite person!' Kara said. 'Leo loves animals . . .'

'Yes, we know . . .'

'. . . but he doesn't like shopping. And he's good, and beautiful, and clever, and . . .'

'Kara!' Mark said. 'We know all this.'

'You talk about him all the time,' Hannah said. 'But now I'm going to ask you three questions about him. Answer the questions, and you can talk about Leonardo every day.'

'But one wrong answer,' Mark said, 'and you can never talk about him again. And we can take your Leonardo posters away from you.'

'Are the questions difficult?' Kara asked.

'For you? Of course they aren't. You love Leonardo,' Mark said.

'You're right. Ask me the questions,' Kara said.

'OK, Kara, here's the first question. What is Leonardo DiCaprio's middle name?' Hannah asked.

Kara answered quickly, 'Wilhelm.'

'That's right,' Hannah said.

'A beautiful name for a beautiful person . . .' Kara said.

'Stop – I'm going to be ill,' Mark said. 'Next

1

question. What film did DiCaprio make with Johnny Depp?'

'*What's Eating Gilbert Grape?*,' Kara answered. 'Leonardo was really good in it, and he . . .'

'We only want the answers,' Mark said. 'But you're right. Now – question number three.' He looked at Hannah.

'OK, Kara,' Hannah said. 'Leonardo made *The Beach* in Thailand, and an animal attacked him there. What was the animal?'

Kara smiled. 'A starfish,' she said.

Hannah looked at the questions and answers. Kara and Mark waited.

'I'm sorry,' Hannah said. 'You're wrong.'

'Yes!' Mark said.

Kara was unhappy. 'What's the right answer?' she asked.

'It was a jellyfish,' Hannah said. 'Look. It's in this newspaper story.'

Mark danced across the room.

'OK, Kara. I'm going to take down your DiCaprio posters,' he said.

'Mark,' Hannah said. 'Kara is our friend. She can have the posters. But, Kara, you can't talk about Leonardo to us.'

'Really? Never?' Kara asked.

'Never!' Mark and Hannah said.

◆

For two weeks Kara didn't talk about her favourite person, but then a poster went up at school.

'I'm sorry,' Hannah said. 'You're wrong.'

WHAT'S HOT?

Television's best programme for young people is looking for one boy and one girl.

Do **YOU** want to be on TV? Then let's talk!
Come to Room B4 at 4.30 on Friday, 7 June.

The winners are going to watch two new films and talk about them on
WHAT'S HOT?
They can also ask the star of one film, Leonardo DiCaprio, questions about his work.

'What?!' Kara said. 'This is amazing! Talk to Leonardo! Be on TV! I'm going to win!'

In Room B4

It was the afternoon of 7 June. There were a lot of boys and girls at the door of Room B4. They all wanted to be on television. Mark and Hannah were there too.

'Kara, are you ready for this?' Hannah asked.

'Yes! I can't wait!' Kara said. 'I'm really excited.'

'Me too!' Mark said. 'I want to be on TV. Every girl in the country is going to see me. They're going to love me.'

A man from *WHAT'S HOT?* opened the door.

'What?!' Kara said. 'This is amazing!'

'Hello! We're ready now. Who's first, please?'

Kara closed her eyes.

'Are you nervous, Kara?' Hannah asked. 'You're going to be really good.'

'We're all going to be good, and I'm going to be a star. A big Hollywood star,' Mark said.

Hannah and Kara smiled.

Kara, Hannah and Mark were at the door now.

'Kara, you go in first,' Hannah said.

'Really?' Kara asked.

'Yes. You're nervous and we aren't,' Hannah said.

The door opened and a girl came out.

'Who's next?' the man asked.

Kara walked slowly into Room B4.

'Hi, I'm Steve,' the man from *WHAT'S HOT?* said. 'And what's your name?'

Suddenly Kara didn't know her name. What was it? 'Kara,' she said. 'It's Kara.'

'Don't be nervous,' Steve said.

He asked a question, but Kara didn't hear him.

'I'm sorry,' she said. 'What did you say?'

'Did you see a film this week?' Steve asked again.

'Yes, I go to the cinema every week,' Kara said. 'Oh, what was the name of the film? I can't remember . . .'

Steve stopped her. 'OK. What's your favourite film?'

'*Titanic*,' Kara said. 'I love it. It's a beautiful story, and Leonardo DiCaprio is amazing in it.'

'You like Leonardo DiCaprio?' Steve asked.

'I love him!' Kara said. 'He's my favourite person.'

'Are you nervous, Kara?' Hannah asked.

Kara talked and talked about her star.

Suddenly Steve said, 'That was very interesting, Kara. Thank you.'

At the door, Kara asked, 'When are we going to know the names of the winners?'

'We're going to telephone them on Monday at about five,' Steve said.

'And do you have my telephone number?' Kara asked. Steve smiled. 'Yes, we have. Thank you.'

Mark was next. He went into the room and Kara talked to Hannah.

'How was it?' Hannah asked.

'Oh, my first answer was very bad. He asked me about Friday's film and I didn't remember the name of it.'

'Oh, it was *Shakespeare in Love*. I loved it. I can talk about that,' Hannah said.

Then Mark came out and Hannah went into the room.

Monday Afternoon

It was 4.45 on Monday afternoon and Kara was in her bedroom. She looked at her posters of Leonardo DiCaprio. His face smiled down at her.

'I'm going to meet you,' she said to him. 'I'm going to talk to you and ask you questions.'

'Kara! Telephone!' It was her mother. 'It's Steve from *WHAT'S HOT?*'

'Hello? Steve? Is it really you?' Kara asked.

'Yes, it's me. Listen. You're our reserve for the programme . . .'

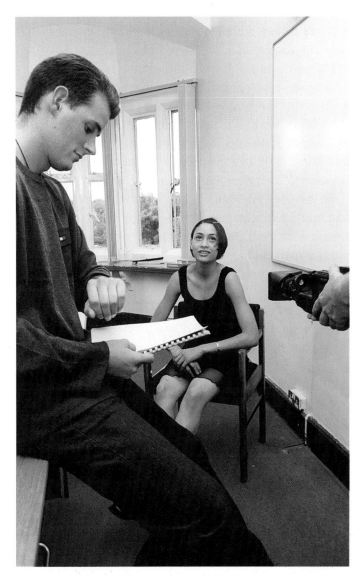

Kara talked and talked about her star.

Steve talked, but Kara didn't listen. Not the winner — only the reserve. She was very unhappy.

'What's wrong?' Kara's mother asked.

'I'm the reserve.'

'But that's very good,' her mother said.

'No, it isn't! I'm not going to meet Leonardo DiCaprio,' Kara said. 'The winners are going to be on television. I'm not going to be on the programme because the winners aren't going to be ill.'

It was the telephone again — Mark this time. 'Did you hear? I'm not going to be a star! Sean's doing the programme. And Hannah did really well,' Mark said.

'Hannah?' Kara asked.

'Didn't she say? She's a winner too,' Mark said.

'Really? I'm going to talk to her now. Goodbye, Mark,' Kara said.

She telephoned her friend.

'Hello? Hannah? It's me, your reserve,' she said. 'You did really well.'

'Thank you, Kara,' Hannah said. 'I'm sorry . . .'

'And you're going to meet Leonardo on Saturday?' Kara asked.

'That's right,' Hannah said quietly. 'And I'm going to talk to him about you.'

Kara said goodbye and went to her bedroom. She was very unhappy.

'I really wanted to meet you,' she said to Leonardo's picture. 'But you're going to meet Hannah.'

But then Kara had an idea.

'What's wrong?' Kara's mother asked.

Kara's Idea

On Friday night Kara walked to Hannah's house. She wanted to ask her friend a very important question.

Hannah opened the door and smiled.

'Hi, Kara. Tomorrow's my big day. I'm really excited.'

'Hannah, can I talk to you?' Kara asked.

'Yes. What's wrong?' Hannah asked.

'You don't really like Leonardo DiCaprio,' Kara said.

'Oh, he's OK. He was good in *Titanic*. Why?'

'Hannah, I love him, and you're my best friend. Can you please be ill tomorrow? I really want to meet Leonardo. Please, Hannah. Do this for me!' Kara said.

Hannah looked at Kara.

'You can't ask that,' she said. 'I want to be on TV. And Steve wants me for the programme.'

'But I helped you!' Kara said.

'What? How?' Hannah asked.

'I didn't answer the first question very well, but you were ready for it. And I went into the room before you. That was *your* idea! I was nervous with Steve, but you weren't,' Kara said.

'Kara, that's not right. You wanted to go in first, and I wanted to help you,' Hannah said.

Kara was very angry. 'I'm going now. Have a good time tomorrow!'

Friends

Hannah didn't sleep on Friday night. Her best friend was angry with her.

'Please, Hannah. Do this for me!' Kara said.

Early in the morning Hannah's mother said, 'Hello, TV star. Are you excited?'

'Oh, yes,' Hannah said. Then suddenly she said, 'But first I'm going to see Kara.'

She walked to her friend's house, and Kara's father opened the door.

'It's very early for a visit, Hannah!' he said.

Kara came down from her bedroom.

'Hannah!'

'Kara, I didn't sleep all night,' Hannah said. 'You're my best friend. I *am* going to be ill today, and you can be on *WHAT'S HOT? You* can meet Leonardo.'

'Hannah! You're going to do this for me?' Kara asked.

'Yes,' Hannah said. 'I want to do it. Friends are important.'

Hannah's mother arrived at Kara's house.

'Hannah, what are you doing?' she said. 'You're going to be late for the programme.'

Hannah started to answer, but Kara said quickly, 'She was nervous, but she's OK now. She's going to be a star today.'

'Really?' Hannah asked her quietly.

Kara said, 'Yes, Hannah, really! You're an amazing friend, but I can't take this away from you.'

'Oh, Kara, thank you,' Hannah said.

'But Hannah,' Kara said. 'Ask Leonardo one question for me. Was it a jellyfish or a starfish in Thailand?'

Hannah smiled and went home with her mother.

Kara closed the door behind her. The TV programme wasn't important; Leonardo DiCaprio wasn't *really* important. But friends – yes, they *were* important.

Leonardo DiCaprio wasn't really important.

ACTIVITIES

Before you read

1 Answer these questions. Find the words in *italics* in your dictionary.

   a Have you got a *best* friend? How does he or she *help* you?

   b When are you *excited*? When are you *nervous*?

   c What is your *favourite* television *programme*?

   d Have you got a *middle* name?

   e When is your *next* English *test*? Are you *ready* for it?

   f Do you have *posters* of film *stars* in your bedroom? Which film stars do you *really* like?

2 Now put these words into the sentences.

   amazing   attack   idea   jellyfish   reserve   starfish   win

   a There are ..... and ..... in the sea near here. Do they ..... people?

   b I've got an ....! Let's go to India!

   c Only one person can be on television. I'm going to ..... and you can be my ....

After you read

3 Answer these questions about the story.

   a Why do Hannah and Mark think of a test for Kara? Is it a good idea?

   b Why is Kara excited about a poster at school?

   c What is Kara's idea?

4 Who is the best friend in the story? Why?

Writing

5 You want to be on *WHAT'S HOT?* Write a letter to Steve. Write about your favourite film.

6 Why are famous people important to young people? Why do they buy posters and books about them?

Answers for the Activities in this book are published in our free resource packs for teachers, the Penguin Readers Factsheets, or available on a separate sheet. Please write to your local Pearson Education office or to: Marketing Department, Penguin Longman Publishing, 5 Bentinck Street, London W1M 5RN.